The Ultimate Playbook

The Ultimate Playbook

For Recruiting & Retaining Real Estate Agents

Andy Goodman

Andy Goodman
The Ultimate Playbook
For Recruiting & Retaining Real Estate Agents

Published by Spines Publishing Platform
ISBN: 979-8-89383-864-0

Contents

Dedication

To my father who helped me discover my "why", my wife Katrina for all her subtle and not so subtle ways she inspires me, my beautiful children Drew, Ava, Corey, Ari and Everly for being my daily "why". A special thanks to the 2021-2022 Coldwell Banker Austin Leadership Team, Floyd Wickman and Team for bringing out my passion for developing people, Keller Williams for their investment in my path.

#love

Foreword

Over the past 30 years, the Real Estate practice is ever changing, it always has and always will, however, never so profoundly as in the last few years for leadership. I remember as an Agent many evolutions ago, before we had the internet and listings were delivered to the office in thick "books" that were shared with all the agents, we used physical maps to find places, no ability to aggregate data on the spot via "Google", we had pagers, no cell phones, etc. The internet was the first major movement and created opportunities for the Real Estate industry to evolve where the ultimate end game in business to "win" was veiled in the progress of the moment. The last few years have presented an acceleration in the technology movement which differs from the former movement as now we are in a race for the top presenting two main challenges for those that will survive. First, the modern Real Estate Agent is empowered in a variety of ways to seek leverage in their value through negotiation with the brokerage. Secondly, because the Agent has leverage, this has caused the brokerage models to shift thus transforming the role of the traditional office manager to a leadership role geared toward a new model, "The Real Estate Agent Acquisition Model."

This "new" Real Estate Acquisition model is centered around growth in a hyper- competitive environment and the profitability of a Real Estate brokerage is often tied to the speed and scale of the ability to attract, retain, and upgrade Real Estate Agent talent by acquiring market share via "productive Agents". In fact, an emphasis on recruitment of talent is the focus of most progressive business models that rely on sales. To that end, the scope and scale of technology is re-writing the Real Estate business model before our very eyes and is presenting new frontiers to navigate and achieve best practices in maintaining/growing a viable Real Estate Company.

Over the last decade, my focus has transitioned from Real Estate sales to teacher/coach to leader of leaders on the corporate side of Real Estate. My passion is helping both Agents and Real Estate leadership by forming trust relationships and finding ways to train the discipline to *do the things people need to do even when they don't want to do it* so they can achieve success in their role and in life.

For Agents, the challenge is helping them thrive in an industry that often has little accountability, an industry where the difference between good and great often has nothing to do with pedigree and background education and more about desire and hustle. On the leadership side, today's leadership needs to learn how to attract, coach and retain Agents in a massively competitive landscape where the industry is moving toward a "winner take all" consolidation, trust me when I tell you that there will be fewer brokerages when the dust settles.

My approach to these challenges and influencing people centers on finding out what's the difference in people, *why do so few get so much in Real Estate and why do so many get so little?* We need to discover the "why" in people and leverage that motivation to change behavior so that uncertainties become certainties for Agents and leaders.

There are many theories that have been broadly uncovered in high achievement psychology and I am not trying with this Playbook to re-spin intellectual capital but rather create new methods of disciplines centered around industry specific foundational psychological absolutes. This "Playbook" is written in respect to all those self-help resources and diced down in an "easy" read, best practice Playbook. With that in mind, this Playbook is a compilation of my 30 years in Real Estate working with some brilliant minds in the industry and decades of being a student, coach, and leader in what is and always will be, a "sales" process.

Warning: If you are reading this Playbook, you are a business leader and a big part of your role and the most critical avenue to achieving success is likely attracting talent. A word of caution, this Playbook is for those in the **leadership mindset vs. the manager mindset**, if you are not familiar with that distinction, it is *important* that you find the difference and *then* jump in! For my leaders out there, if you internalize these concepts and develop habits, you will experience a personal evolution that will change the way you communicate. Enjoy the journey, this is your road to developing a powerful emotional IQ which will positively impact all aspects of your life.

Welcome to the most comprehensive and straight to the point best practices "Playbook" designed for leadership to recruit and retain top Agent talent! My goal is to make broad concepts *"easy"* as my style is more execution vs. over analysis. Your "Playbook" is meant to evolve as you do, each section is to be viewed as baseline components which will become *personal* best practices as you master each discipline and establish your "brand". Each chapter has definitions which are common words that take on new meanings indigenous to this playbook as well as sections meant to be used as a "workbook". Look for throughout:

"Expert Tips"

These *"tips"* represent <u>absolute methods</u> for getting results.

Welcome.

Road to Mastery:
Develop your "Brand"

"A laborer works with their hands, a craftsman works with their hands and head, a Master works with their hands, head and heart."

— *Unknown*

Your "brand" is the ultimate growth achievement in the recruitment role as you go from the "hunter" to the "gatherer". In other words, when you have reached a high level of attraction as a leader and growth facilitator, Agents will recognize you as a leader in your role and seek you out for consultation and/or agree to meet with *less effort*. This is the same concept that exists for your top Agents, they are recognized for their talent and people want to work with them. The key for you is to build your brand through visibility in a way that positions you as a local leader with a *mystic* that attracts interest.

Best practices to build your "brand" visibility:

- **Drop in open houses to meet Agents**
- **Attend local Realtor events**
- **Join business to business groups**
- **Advertise in public directories such as school**
- **Sponsor Events**
- **Have a dedicated branded social media page highlighting what your brand**
- **Blog**
- **Start a "youtube" channel with short weekly videos providing coaching tips**

Expert Tip: The key to social media, especially youtube, is consistency. You need to post every week at least one video. Look for cost effective video editing tools to expedite the editing time, pre-plan content and invest in a microphone, ring light, etc.

What are other areas that you can make yourself visible/build your brand?

____

____

The Mindset of a High Achiever

The best athletes, performers, business- people all have one thing in common, they play an **<u>internal game.</u>** If you ask high achievers who they compete against, it is generally not another competitor, they tend to compete against *what's possible.* <u>All</u> high achievers develop simple "baseline" habits such as morning routines, avoiding detours (time-suckers: activities that don't contribute to the goal) and are *self-disciplined* to stay consistent on their best use of their time. For you to be on the road to high achievement in your role, you need to absolutely do/have the following:

- **Time-blocked, non-negotiable prospecting:** You *must* build a wall, ceiling, and floor around this activity. You will have plenty of time to address the "stuff" which we will refer to as the normal "problems" that will *always* exist in your day- to- day business. *Without mastery of time-blocking, the effectiveness of everything else you do will be severely marginalized.*

- **Big Vision, Big Why, Big Goals:** If you are in your role and the salary meets your needs to the extent that you can accomplish what you want to in life, *being a recruiter could be the wrong role for you.* High level achievers in *the recruiter* role <u>*live in the bonus structure*</u> to fuel their Big Vision. *We will help you discover your "Why" in subsequent chapters.*

- **The Right Personality Profile:** If your core personality leads with analytical thinking (you need things to be black and white) this role will be more of a challenge. High achievers in this role profile as executers *with* "high emotional IQ's", they read people well and expertly pace themselves in conversations, they are very purposeful in their focus and do not get slowed down by the details.

  Example: *Big picture thinkers vs. everything needs to be correct thinkers*

- **Contribution Based:** You internally and authentically get a high level of satisfaction from other people reaching their potential.

Briefly Describe something "contribution-based" that you have accomplished in your life:

____

____

The reason why making appointments stick via cold calls can be challenging is because the Agent we are calling doesn't *feel* like it's important enough to meet you, they don't see the opportunity to gain. For instance, if you are calling successful Agents, *high achievers have a big fear of their time being wasted as their time comes at a high price.* The question becomes, what script do I need to make meeting with me *valuable*?

Let's face it, if an Agent had the opportunity to go on a *million-dollar listing appointment,* they would have no issues finding time in their schedule to attend. Think about what a "million-dollar" listing represents to an Agent, it is an opportunity to gain with no guarantees, an Agent will drop everything every time for that chance! When you master the technique to set appointments with an opportunity to gain in the eyes of the prospect, you will begin to set appointments at a high level. We can help you with that in later chapters but for now, I need you to answer two questions and paste the answers on a wall near your desk and read each statement with purpose before your daily prospecting session:

The Million-Dollar Listing

"High achievers have the ability to do the things they know they should do, even when they don't want to do it."

— *Nick Saban*

The high achievers in recruiting adopt a mindset that "plays" the numbers game. In fact, almost all successful businesses don't worry as much about the rejection factor and focus on the conversion ratio. The secret of successful recruiters is that they are religious about <u>time-blocking and making contacts</u>. Remember, survival is human nature, thriving (high achievement) is not fundamental to human nature.

To achieve at the highest level, it is imperative that you find discipline in your daily routine to sometimes "do activities that you don't feel like doing" because these activities ultimately fuel your big goals. A baseline skill is to master the phone and frankly, deal effectively with call reluctance through mindset. Call reluctance is when the phone feels like 1,000 pounds, see "why do I prospect" (page 19).

- **<u>Why I prospect</u>**. Write a statement that describes what results from prospecting mean in your life. *Does it make you feel successful? Does it help you earn more money to achieve goals for your family? Are you fiercely competitive and need to win?* (Go deep and get personal with yourself, be selfish, there are no wrong answers, it is what motivates you!)

Write a brief statement below on *why* you prospect:

____

____

- **<u>Who am I calling?</u>** *Are these strangers that need your help? Are they people that don't know they need your help? Do these Agents need your help? Why?*

Write a brief statement that describes who is on the other end of the line on a cold call:

____

____

Time Blocking

"If you can't control your time (in business), nothing else matters."

— *Floyd Wickman*

The key to becoming a successful recruiter, growth facilitator and influencer in life is to have conversations daily with prospects. It is *simple* but not *easy*. Human nature dictates that prospecting some days is completely effortless and some days it is a struggle. The secret is to make it organic, a simple extension of a daily habit such as brushing your teeth. What often derails a good prospecting routine is the preparation and mindset. A best practice for developing good prospecting habits:

Time block: You need to block 2 hours daily in the morning (first thing) where you can go from your car to your desk with a list of prospects that was <u>prepared in advance</u>, either through administrative leverage or you *before* the close of business on the previous day.

Expert Tip: **Color coded calendar**

Green = recruiting appointments &

prospecting sessions

Yellow = meetings/training, coaching,

solving business problems, etc.

Pink = personal

M	TU	W	TH	F	S	S
Lead Gen	Lead Gen	Lead Gen	Day off	Lead Gen	Flex Time	Spend quality time with your family
Database building/social media posts	Office meeting	Training at office	Day off	Flex Time	Flex Time	Open House
Personal Time	Office Meeting	Home Inspection	Day off	Social media Training	Return calls	Open House
Networking group	Return calls/Prepare for next day	List Appt	Day off	Listing Appt	Flex Time	Personal
Return calls/set appts/prepare for next day	Listing Appt.	Flex Time	Day off	Return calls/prepare for weekend	Flex Time	Personal

Leveraged Prospecting Resources

"Everything we want in life is outside our comfort zone."

— *Multiple*

If preparation creates separation, *"who am I calling?"* is the goal of proper preparation. A big puzzle piece in your journey toward success will be creating leveraged sources of leads and developing a systemized approach for establishing a pipeline so each prospecting session can be concentrated on making contacts vs. finding contacts.

Best prospect resources:

1. <u>Agents with a local competitor:</u> have your admin print out lists of local offices with the Agent's name, cell, Real Estate Company, and approximate GCI from the previous 12 months. *You should have a big pool of lists that you can rotate through.
2. <u>Co-op lists</u>: *prepared by your admin* (usually good for one session every week).

For other sources of prospects, it is a mix between easy (low rejection factor) and difficult (higher rejection factor). The more difficult involves more "guts" and as you already know, <u>the "guts" calls yield the highest results.</u>

The use of the **"Risk-Reward Calculator"** (below) will ensure that your prospect sources are a healthy mix. Secondary resources include:

Agents holding open houses |referrals from your Agents| cold calls| Agents who left your brokerage| Agents that *just* left their brokerage

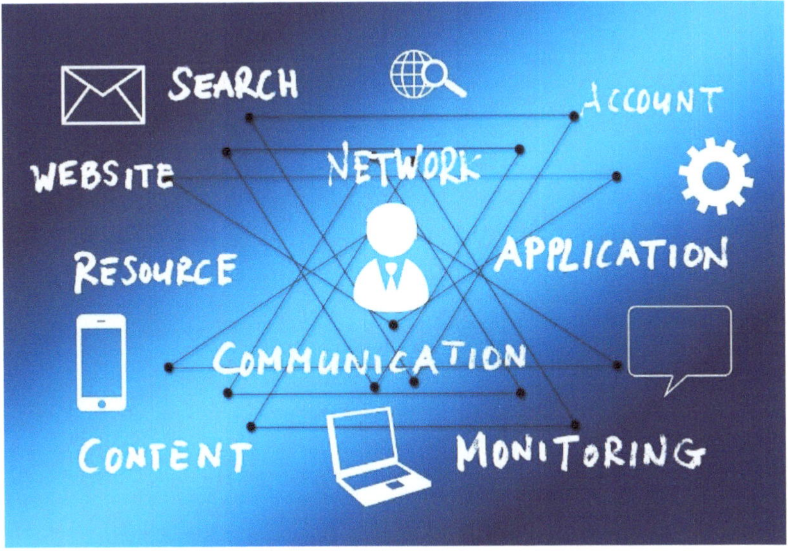

Once you have the prospect identified, the next step is "run" it through the **Risk-Reward Calculator**:

Risk-Reward Calculator

No risk---------------------------------High Reward

1 2 3 4 5 6 7 8 9 10

Source Value

Allied Resources (vendors) -1

RE-Schools -2

Social Media -3

Employment Ads -4

Open Houses -5

General Public -6

Friends & Family -7

Agent Referrals -8

Agents that just left their Company -9

Cold Calls -10

Expert Tip: Anything short of a voice to voice reduces the chances of getting a result by 89%. Don't bet against this percentage!

5-Point Valid Appointment Qualifier

"The biggest leadership challenge is working with people who don't want a big life."

— *John Maxwell*

The challenge with setting a high level of appointments is the ability to set appointments <u>who show up!</u> Lack of standards relating to what constitutes a truly "valid" appointment is the difference between a high conversion rate and a high failure rate. Think of it this way, if you are selling Real Estate or anything for that matter, not having both spouses present, enough time to close, clear motivation, etc. is a set-up for failure. The secret to a high level of success is to have non-negotiable standards so that you have the clearest path to close. The <u>definition of a valid appointment</u>: An appointment set with the obstacles removed that would typically prevent the prospect from reaching a decision.

The 5 Point Qualifier for best odds for success:

1. Willing to <u>meet at the office</u> vs. meet at a coffee shop/restaurant.
2. Willing to <u>spend the time</u> to allow you to present vs. a "drive by" appointment.
3. Willing to <u>Disclose details</u> about their business vs. won't allow themselves to be vulnerable in your discovery questions.
4. <u>All decision makers present</u> vs. team members that won't attend.
5. <u>Motivated to grow</u> vs. just can't say "no" over the phone.

Expert Tip: Great way to get an Agent to open up, ask an Agent prospect, *"Do you feel you have reached your full potential?"*

Once the prospect has met your "valid" appointment standards, they agree to a meeting at your office with all decision makers present, enough time and an opportunity to gain mindset, the next step is to prepare for a winning consultation!

Preparing for the Consultation

"Trust the process."

— *Sam Hinkie, former Philadelphia 76ers GM*

The next step is to convert a "valid" appointment from curious, "just looking," to a "I didn't realize, and I must make a change" mindset. The key is to follow a <u>process</u>, let the process *get it* for you or help *you or lose it* quicker *thus your time* becomes more valuable! Preparation is the key to increasing your odds of success.

Gather intel: Compile production data for the last 24 months to include units sold, sales volume, buyer vs. listing sales, average sale price and average commission rate. Your data should start to tell a story and should answer:

- Is their business growing, declining or flat?
- Average sales price and commission rate
- Buyer to Seller ratio
- Total number of transactions annually
- Current listings/sales

Expert Tip: Review candidate's social media, branding, and overall online presence.

The Ultimate Consultation & The Great Set-Up

"Fear of loss is a greater motivator than opportunity to gain."

— *Multiple*

Generally, prospects can either be closed in one or two appointments, this process is referred to as the "one-step" or "two-step" process as follows:

<u>One-Step:</u> Meets valid appointment criteria (prospect has a clear path to decision)

<u>Two-Step:</u> Does not meet (or unsure) if it meets valid appointment criteria.

Caution: A two-step can turn into a one-step so always be prepared! In fact, the better you become, you will be able to flip two's into one's!

The Purpose of the **One** or **Two-Step** approach is the same, *gain leverage*. If it is a "**Two-Step**", the leverage should position you for a *quick* follow up meeting with perhaps another member on your team or additional support (technology person, other person of influence).

Appointment Goals:

- **Follow a process:** Stay disciplined to the process.
- **Build rapport**: Ask them *why* it is important for them to be successful, hunt for something in their past that motivates them, *if they express emotion, you hit their motivation! Use their motivation as leverage. *Limit selling your Company and you, they should do 90% of the talking). Take notes where appropriate.
- **Discover their "why"**: What is most important to them right now.
- **Gain leverage**: Find a problem/pain point in their business.
- **Monetize their Loss**: Tie their admitted shortcoming in their business to the number of transactions (expressed as the number of lost deals multiplied by their average commission) and show them how it subtracts from their big "why."
- **Get a Conviction**: This is the process where they admit there is a hole that needs to be filled and it is impacting what's most important to them and solving this is a "must."
- **Close to a Commitment**: Follow the closing process.

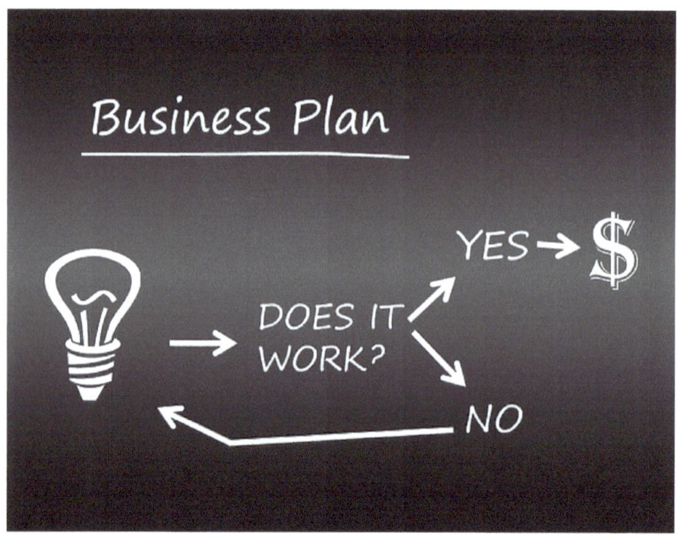

The Great Set-Up: The Great Set-Up is a process of leverage where the skilled recruiter disarms the prospect by changing the opportunity to gain achieved when setting up the appointment with an opening statement that conveys a fear of loss. In other words, the prospect showed up because you convinced them of a benefit, however, through your "Set-Up" statement, you make it clear that this meeting is more of a fact-finding session. You now have more leverage in the consultation because the "Set-Up" statement repositions you from the recruiter to a valuable and neutral (at this juncture) business consultant.

Expert Tip: Role play! The best performers practice their skills, a baseball player takes practice swings in the batter's circle, an opera singer does the note scale, actors rehearse lines in the mirror. Don't expect to be great without rehearsal and practice with your leadership group.

 *Expert Tip:* Create an inviting experience for the Agent, have staff greet by name, lead Agent candidate to a room with a window, have your computer set-up to present in advance, have your questions/business analysis sheet ready to go, it's **SHOWTIME!**

Start with a **Take-away statement** (Fear of loss), change the appointment from being nervous about the result to letting the prospect know that this is an opportunity that may or may not be offered:

"I don't want to recruit you for the sake of recruiting an agent. Frankly, if we can't establish trust that I can help you and establish rapport, we shouldn't work together no matter how much I can offer, don't you agree? So, in order to avoid failure in our time together I have a process which works like this……."

1. *Can I have permission to ask you some questions?*
2. *If we find an opportunity to improve your business, can I share it?*
3. *If we agree on a challenge, can I propose a solution?*
4. *If you feel the solution could impact your business in a meaningful way and I feel I could make it happen, we can then mutually agree to explore what the solution would entail.*
5. *Lastly, if we get to a point where things make major sense, we can contrast any challenges and talk timing and details, sound good?*

If you find that a proposed solution(s) is meaningful to your business and I feel that I can make it happen, we can talk about what that looks like but for now, I just want to see where your business is trending. You work for a good Company and naturally there are things our Company is that your company is not and there are things your company is that we are not, my goal in our brief time together is to see if the things that we are that you Company is not add up to a substantial difference. If not, I will give you whatever advice I can to help you on your journey and most likely will recommend you stay the course, fair enough? (your tone should be calm and matter of fact)

Once they agree with the process, begin on discovering their "*big why*" and understanding their value system through questions (Appendix A). <u>The skill is to find something they are emotional about and the reason that they NEED to succeed and use questions to plant seeds of doubt in the certainty of their current business process.</u> If an Agent's biggest fear is uncertainty, you have everything you need to take this all the way through to an affiliation. Remember, *all* Realtors have holes in their business because sadly, most Agents don't run their business like a business! Asking the right questions will help them self-discover these opportunities and position you as someone who can help them with their business. Moreover, through meaningful questions, you will establish a strong trust bond and be able to present solutions that demonstrate what they are doing yield inadequate results relating to their life purpose. When they see this clearly, you have achieved leverage in the process and will be moving toward a successful partnership with the Agent!

Expert Tip: Results become obtainable when you bridge a series of admissions that lead to a <u>conviction statement</u>.

Cross Examine: Ask strategic and leading questions to find areas where they self-discover holes in their business. Ask "scale from one to ten" questions such as *"On a scale from one to ten, how effective is your database?"*

Expert Tip: Resist the urge to comment and discuss after asking questions, stay in curiosity.

Keep in mind that ALL realtors that will take a meeting with you have *massive holes* in their business and opportunities to make more money or make the same money in less time. *The Agents that are wildly successful to the degree where they have mastered leverage and profitability are a small subset.

*See Appendix A for high leverage questions

Expert Tip: Agents that meet with you, even the ones that appear "successful" have imperfect businesses.

<u>Get THEIR number</u>: Let them *tell you* how many deals *they* feel they could do if they improved___________ (insert the stated problem you revealed through your discovery questions).

Example: "So if your database was improved from a 4 to a 7, how many extra transactions do you think you could do?"

"So if I took_____________ (number of extra transactions) and multiplied it by your average commission _________________ (insert average commission), we are talking about _____________ (should be a substantial number) *Present the number with enthusiasm and you need to see an excited reaction from the prospect, if not, either the number isn't big enough or they don't believe they can do it. If so, go back and keep asking questions and make sure that the "why" you discovered is truly what motivates them."

<u>Eliminate the Pain</u> (For 2-step) Meet again and for 2nd session, prepare a customized plan and close with massive leverage by showing how the plan will <u>create a clear and compelling future</u>. *The solutions are the application of your technology platform, coaching, training, and tools where the Agent prospect can clearly see. End your presentation by tying the solution to their big "why".

Expert Tip: Once confidence in the solution is achieved, re-state their total recurring annual lost income as monthly loss.

<u>Get a conviction</u>: Use a "If we could, would you statement."
"If I could show you a way not to lose _______($) every month by creating a system that does _________ so you can generate _______ more deals (insert the number they told you), so you could achieve __________(insert their big "why") would that be something that would be powerful enough to move your business?

"Find what's truly important to someone and the impossible becomes non-negotiable."

—ALG

Deconstructing the Consultation

Let's Deconstruct the Elements in the Process of the Ultimate Consultation:

Initial consultation: Standard business analysis questions (pre-prepared), interviewer (you) needs to be in a peak mental state, gain rapport, discover predominant human needs, values and big "why" (next section).

Ask business questions purposefully: When they answer, *resist urge to talk*, stay out of judgement, stay in curiosity. Keep comments short, reassuring, positive and confident.

Look for a hot button: Predominant area you can improve if they were presented with the right tools, systems that *they acknowledge* is a short fall in their business.

<u>They</u> Self-Discover and Provide <u>Their Number</u> of additional transactions they could obtain by improving their admitted hole in their business.

*This is really important that the number comes from them.

<u>Do not discuss solutions</u> to their problems or share solutions <u>in step one of two-step</u>.

If converting to a "two-step", remain poised and confident. Ask the prospect to schedule a follow-up appointment with you right there on the spot no later than another day or two.

*Be very careful not to discuss compensation or any other benefits, you need to hold something back so that they have a reason to meet.

Gaining Emotional Leverage: Finding Their "Why"

"People don't care what you think unless they know you care about them."

— *Zig Zigler*

The Zig Zigler quote is one of the classic quotes that sheds light on the skill required to build rapport and gain influence. In the recruiting process, unless you establish trust and rapport, a relationship that leads to a result will never develop. One major challenge to rapport building in the recruiting process is something called "**Controlled Curiosity**" which is the ability to limit the "life story" often Agents want to tell and/or their desire to gain significance. Agents by nature tend to be highly social and will attempt to control the conversation, serving as an unconscious effort to create an obstacle for you to find a pain point. Through **Controlled Curiosity,** ask questions that steer the conversation back on track at multiple junctures to keep the focus on two predominant aspects:

1. *Why it is important for them to succeed?*
2. *What will happen if they don't achieve success (fear of loss)?*

In depth Rapport Building requires execution of two main skills/ techniques:

1. Trust bonding
2. Understanding **The Basic human needs**:

Certainty-The need to feel safe and comfortable.

Variety-The need for physical and mental stimulation.

Love & Connection-The need to be loved and connected to others.

Growth-The need to develop and expand.

Contribution-The need to contribute beyond yourself.

Let's try a brief exercise to discover _your_ primary needs.......

What is most important in your life right now?

____

____

Why is that important?

____

____

What else is important?

____

____

Why is that so important to you?

____

____

Tell me more about that?

____

____

Did you discover that answering these questions led to a powerful drive in your life? If you can take an Agent deep, 4 to 6 "why's", you have identified what is most important to them and positioned yourself as someone who cares and now have permission to present a solution.

Expert Tip: The absence of helping someone gain clarity is the difference between a conversation and creating momentum that has leverage.

Reach an agreement from the agent that a problem exists and not addressing the problem with meaningful action will result in a level of income/opportunity which will impact what is most important to them in life (big "why"). In other words, people don't accomplish significant things unless they have a big "why" (life purpose or vision the person is passionate about) In terms of basic human behavior, survival in instinctive, thriving requires deeper motivation.

Expert Tip: Find the "Big Why" Six levels deep.

"What is the most important reason you want to be successful? Why is that important? Why is that important?........Why is that important?........
**Please understand, this gets uncomfortable for both the interviewer and the candidate, the key from the interviewer side is to calmly press on, be firm but sensitive. When properly executed, the walls will come down between you and the candidate and a powerful bond will start to take shape.*

While they are answering, try to determine if the person fits in **one of two types of values-patterns:**

1. Someone who moves towards values.
2. Someone who moves away from values.

Examples of values people move toward: happiness, love, passion, success, gratitude, energy, security.

Examples of values people move away from: rejection, failure, being alone, anger, depression, sadness, boredom, anxiety, guilt, overwhelmed.

Your Questions need to determine values/patterns in their lives:

Which values do they work hardest to experience?

Which values do they work hardest to avoid?

Get a Conviction & Bridge Building

"Failure hurts when you are too close to it, not as bad when you look at it higher up."

— unknown

Definition of Conviction: A conviction statement is when a prospect admits with *absolute certainty* that something is missing and that they recognize your presented tool (Company Technology) as a solution.

Example: *"Great, I am glad you agree our Social Media Engine (tool) will help you get the 5 extra transactions you need to fund (big why). Let's move toward setting that up for you, fair enough?"*

Definition of Bridge Building: A statement that takes a conviction to an action plan.

Conviction/Bridge Building Summary: Reach an agreement from the agent that a problem exists and not addressing the problem with meaningful action will result in a level of income/opportunity which will impact what is most important to them in life (big "why").

The bridge is the definitive statement that strikes an agreement with the candidate that your action plan, technology or tool will be the solution that will close the gap between their current production and stated goals.

Example:*"If I can show you how to solve your social media gap in your business through our Social Media Engine tool and it resulted in 5 extra transactions, would that be something you need to move towards?"*

Tie-Down Conviction Statement: When you take a weak agreement after a closing question and strengthen it by seeking a stronger conviction that shows a level of passion.

Example: *"You stated that if you could implement ___________(tool) you could do_________(number of stated transactions) and that would create______(dollar value expressed monthly)* which would help you achieve_____________(their big "why")? *Wow, that would be huge, don't you agree?"*

Building your Bridge: *"It looks like we have an opportunity here, may I show you the process that all successful agents use that have upgraded to our Company? Keep in mind, just like you, many of these Agents have pending deals and complicated systems but the good news is, our process makes this relatively painless! The result will be the benefit of earning __________ (monthly amount of income they stated from the number of extra transactions), this will far outweigh any extra energy required on your end, don't you agree?"*

Most Agents predominantly lead with social personalities (*emotional*); however, it is important that your closing technique includes steps that show the less common (*analytical)* Agent you have a process, or you will encounter hesitation. Read on.

Closing with the Soft-Landing Approach

"Be passionate, eliminate distractions, create momentum, fear nothing."

— Andy Reid

The **"Set-Up"** for the final close: *"In order to help you achieve ______________(re-state the number of transactions in an annual whole dollar amount that will result in the adoption of the tool or technology), we have a painless process that offers little set back, in fact, if executed per our* **Soft Landing Program**, *you will be ahead of your current business at every turn. Are you ready!"*

Re-affirm the agreement with a conviction statement that they have made the decision to move and tie down with an assumptive bridge statement.

Example: *Great, congratulations! I am so happy for you! To make this go smoothly, we have what I mentioned, a Soft-Landing Program, this is what all top agents like yourself follow to minimize any challenges. We need to follow these 5 steps precisely and in the exact order for this transition to be successful, fair enough?*

1. Current business: Discover all active and pending and present the "win" of joining your organization clearly as a gain that outweighs any perceived loss. (Focus on long view)
2. Coach them on a script to assure current clients that the move will not jeopardize anything in their current transaction.
3. Review with them the Independent Contractor's Agreement and any perks offered by you to make sure it aligns with their expectations as per your discussions and execute agreement.
4. Provide a script to inform their current broker.
5. Schedule the first orientation and order business cards *before* they leave your office.

Example Script to Inform Former Broker: *"Thank you for the opportunity to work with your Company, however, I have recently decided to make a change to a new brokerage, please understand that I have taken this decision very seriously and need to make this move for the benefit of my career and ultimately my family. I hope the door is open and I would like to sincerely thank you for everything."*

*The most critical step in the process is making sure they do not go to "step #5" *before* any of the other steps, they must notify their broker *after* everything else has been completed, including signing your Independent Contractor's Agreement.

<u>Deal Killers, make sure you don't:</u>

- <u>Let them talk with their broker first</u> (if they are sold, this will not be a challenge)
- <u>Overtalk and oversell</u> the Company after you get your conviction agreement.
- <u>Bring other people into</u> the conversation without them knowing what you are doing.
- <u>Drag the process out</u> by scheduling the process into the future.
- <u>Send paperwork</u> vs. doing it with them.

Re-enforce the move: Best Practices:

- Celebrate quickly with social media/business announcement
- Order cards/sign riders
- On board within 3 days
- Check-in regularly

The Retention Ratio

"When you hire the right people, they thank you, when you hire the wrong people, they blame you."

— GK

Let's start with some **scary numbers**:

91% fail out of the business.

44% in the MLS are earning a poverty level income.

97% of Real Estate Agents don't have an exit strategy.

87% of Top Agents don't lead generate on a consistent basis.

20% of Agents will be out of the business in a shifted market.

So, if we know the failure rates are extraordinary, we know that most Agent's do not operate a disciplined business, they rarely lead generate on a consistent basis, they don't tap into resources, etc., the question becomes (in most instances), *who is failing who?*

Ask your own better producers and see how committed they are to having a high functioning database, prospecting, exit strategy, leverage in their business and overwhelmingly you will discover Agents are often successful *despite* themselves. *What does this tell you about the Agent that is struggling? Is their lack of progress due to something you or your Company has done to them?* Assuming we as leaders aren't neglecting our Agents and in the hopefully rare instances where we are, is it ever a 50-50 problem? 50% of their effort and 50% the Company failed them? How about 60-40 or 70-30……does that make sense?

What makes abundant success based on decades of evidence is that the ratio is closer to 90-10! In other words, you have relatively much less in your control than they do to be successful.

The Ratio Method

Working under the premise that the percentage is around 90% Agent effort and 10% company. Think of it this way, 90% of first year agents fail out of the business in the first 2 years, out of the thousands of Agents in the MLS, 80% are earning less than an optimal income. *Why is that? Is it that 80-90% of the Companies are terrible or is more likely that only 10-20% of the Agents engage on a reasonable level required to run a successful business?* The *fatal flaw* in retention is when the Agent goes into the retention interview thinking it's a 50-50 ratio and we need to make up the percentage by overselling our Company and/or throwing out financial concessions for them to stay.

Golden Formula: Ask questions, find a problem, re-calibrate the ratio's in their mind.

The retention dilemma states that it is easier for the agent to deflect vs. take responsibility for shortcomings in their business. We know as leaders, "hustle" cures a lot of ills for Agents and when you look forensically at a typical Agent's effort/engagement, you will see plenty of evidence pointing to the true issue. The **Ratio Method** is the tool to recalibrate from 50-50 to closer to the correct ratio of 90-10 by "re-recruiting" the Agent through the process in your Playbook. **Ask discovery questions, discover their "why", propose a solution, get a conviction, build a bridge and close.**

The Ratio Method Elements:

- <u>Re-recruit/interview</u> the Agent as if they were with another Company, follow the exact process outlined in earlier sections (find the "why" and ask questions).
- Get them to <u>self-discover/admit</u> that they do not take advantage of tools, systems, etc.
- <u>Monetize</u> the gap in their business by letting them tell you how many transactions they could realize if they engaged with a specific tool.
- <u>Get a conviction,</u> build a bridge, and close.

Expert Tip: Sell the disruption of change if they are determined to take their business to another firm and get them to commit to a "trial" period to "fix" elements in their business with a specific action plan.

Exercise: Examine at the make-up of your office, are you rich in heavy producers or do you attract a lot of similar agents of lower production? The fact is that we tend to attract people who are like us, the key with retention is to be "enough" for the top producers through consultive relationship. Write down the names of 5 Agents you need to strengthen your relationship with:

1.

2.

3.

4.

5.

Expert Tip: You need a consultative relationship with your Agents which is not necessarily about being their friend, seek to be "respected" vs. being "liked". You gain respect by understanding their business and coaching through solutions.

Key points to remember with Retention:

<u>People want significance</u>, the fact of the matter is, being a realtor is a straight commission gig and takes some guts and even the smallest level of accomplishment is a big thing to agents. The retention skill is to NEVER let people slip below the radar by having retention systems in place, this should be a leveraged whole year system vs. a fire drill once an Agent becomes vulnerable.

Agents generally don't leave if <u>they are making money</u> and <u>feeling significant.</u>

Exercise: Analyze your top producer and compare numbers from this year to the previous and look for something that is "off in terms of a % decrease" in their business and use it a coaching opportunity. The result will be that the Agent will be very impressed that you are paying attention to the trends in their business, and it will position you as that consultive expert that you seek with your top producers. *If top producers view you as someone that understands their business, recruiting efforts by others will be difficult to overcome your relationship.

Top Producer ________________________

Gap in ___________________________ year over year.

Retention-Awareness, Leverage and Consistency

"Change your mindset, change your results."

— Unknown

In general, people don't leave you if they are making money, the relationship with you is often secondary. Top retainers in leadership have a heightened awareness of their Agents patterns, moods, and overall communication style. Agents/people tend to be creatures of habit, they greet you the same way every time they come into the office, their mood is similar in your office meetings, they have the same routines. Top retainers in leadership pay attention to these patterns and they know if something is "off."

Best Practices for Retention:

- Color code roster with green being top 20%, yellow being middle and red being the lower 30%.
- Work with staff on a consistent plan (throughout the year) targeting color coded categories.
- Identify "Retention Season" for you (typically toward the end of the year) & double down.
- Create a "Red Alert" system for identifying vulnerable Agents and quick plan of action.
- Express gratitude in a variety of ways throughout the year in a creative manner.
- Always seek to upgrade your relationships with top producers through consultation.

Diffusing contentious situations:

- In <u>office disputes</u>, don't be the "Dual Agent", rather set the situation up where you remove yourself and the Company from the issue and position yourself as a mediator.
- In <u>conflicts against the Company and/or transactions</u>, position the Company as the vehicle (car), explain we are responsible for the tools and maintenance, the Agent is the driver and they are responsible for how fast they want to drive, who they put in the car with them and what conditions they drive.
- Talk in ratios in your <u>retention conversations</u>, *"What percentage do you see your role in the success of your business and what percentage is the Company's?"*
- Seek win-win outcomes by always talking in terms of solutions *"If we could, would you?"*

Expert Tip: The secret to a great leader, coach, retainer, and recruiter is in the approach to the fact that Agents fail for a myriad of reasons which have little to do with your Company. Play the 10% game, keep in mind that our competitors do things well too and have their flaws as well, it becomes impossible to position the incremental shifts/benefits that lead to extraordinary results when the Agent's mindset is that we own 50% of their success.

Final Thoughts

Congratulations on completing the Playbook, my sincere hope is that you found a deeper understanding, enhanced your technique and feel inspired to take action!

Entertainment vs. Inspiration factor:

- After reading this book, whether large or small, you to do something differently to bring you closer to your goals, then I "*inspired*" you.
- After reading this book, although you may think differently in the moment and even feel *"inspired"*, *without action*, I have "*entertained*" you.

Write down 3 concepts you will commit to executing from the Playbook:

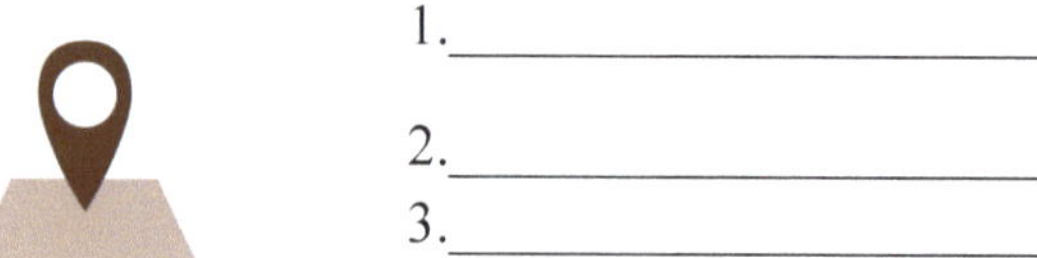

1.______________________________

2.______________________________

3.______________________________

In Conclusion

This is now your Playbook, stay true to the principles and add creativity *only* after achieving results. I close my emails to my leaders/managers with this message:

"To provide the leadership to build relationships to help people take advantage of their opportunities and make sure they have the discipline to do it. I ask only one thing from everyone: each week, come back to me stronger."

#love #youinspireme

About the Author

Humble note about the author: Andy Goodman started in Real Estate as a New Construction salesperson in 1995 and eventually became a top re-sale Agent in a large Pennsylvania market. Andy teamed up with industry legend and Real Estate Agent coaching pioneer, Floyd Wickman and spent several years training and developing Real Estate Agents throughout the country. In 2013, Andy became a Team Leader with Keller Williams in a Philadelphia suburb and set recruiting records in both volume and profit leading to new Company bench-marks for what became possible in the field. Andy joined Coldwell Banker as Regional Vice President in 2021 and helped his leadership team recruit over 500 million in GCI in less than a year. In 2024 Andy joined Leader's Edge Training as an executive Real Estate coach and has developed cutting edge programs: "Recruiting Solutions" & "Retention Solutions" and currently speaks throughout the United States and Canada inspiring Real Estate leaders.

Appendix A:
High Leverage Discovery Questions

Begin with **"The Great Set-Up"** & follow with:

How would you describe your business, growing, maintaining, or declining?

How many transactions is your goal for the next 12 months? Are you on track?

Where do most of your clients come from?

What is the size of your database? Do you market consistently to your database?

"On a scale from 1 to 10, "1" being your database is a hot mess and "10" being it's running at an extremely high level, you are able to track and generate leads on a consistent basis, you have deep data on all your clients and prospects, you are able to see what people are looking at when they engage, where do you think you are?"

"What CRM do you use? Do you like it? Do you feel you are getting the most out of it? (Why or can you describe?). How would you describe your grasp on technology?"

"If you could waive a magic wand and fix one area in your business, what would that be?"

"Are there areas in technology such as lead generation that you don't connect the dots as well as you would like to?"

"Tell me about your lead generation, do you consistently generate leads? How do you prospect? Scale from 1 to 10, "1" being you rarely prospect "10" being you time-block two hours a day each morning and work the phones, where do you fit?"

"How would you describe your current management group…….. competing or solely there to coach and develop?"

"Does your leadership reach out to you and show an active interest in your numbers, coach and develop you or is the relationship where they are available when you have a question but aren't particularly proactive?"

"What areas would you like to see training in your current company that does not exist?"

"What is more important to you, more business (money) or the same amount of business in less time?"

"How would you describe the $10 an hour work in your business?"

"How would you describe the $200 + hour work in your business?"

"What type of leverage do you currently have in your business? Who does the stuff?"

"What are you spending money on that your Company doesn't provide?"

"What is most important to you in your life right now? (doesn't have to be Business) Why is that important? Do you feel your business is positioned to help you with those goals?"

"Do you worry about the certainty of your business, or do you expect that you will do at least as well every year? Why?"

"Do you feel you have reached your full potential? (Scale from 1 to 10 question)"

"How many extra transactions do you feel you could do if you ___________ (stated problem) was running at a higher level?"

Sample Close:

"Based on what you have told me, what I hear you saying is that you are challenged in these main areas (recite from notes) and you admitted that it adds up to _________ additional transactions which is around ________ a year which is by numbers roughly ________ a month. Wow, that's a pretty big number, would you agree?"

Appendix B: Recruiting Scripts

In person

Don't try to be everything, simply find if the differences between what your Company offers that they don't have adds up to a benefit for them. For instance, size of office, support/tech, etc. For instance, size of office, support/tech, etc. Break down each difference and seek a <u>conviction</u>.

Example Script: *"Your office has 300 people and ours has 85, can you see any benefit to being 1 of 85 vs. 1 of 300? If I can show you why you can succeed in a more intimate setting and be more productive, would that have value to you?"*

Show the value and __get a conviction__ after each point vs. overselling, for instance: *"At 85 Agents, we still are large enough to have a huge market share, more attention from non-competing leadership, less distraction from a never ending influx of new agents and better per person production. If all things being equal, do you see the advantage?"* **GET A FIRM YES** (conviction) and then move on to the next difference.

Conversely, if your office is larger, position the benefits of the enhanced market share and collaborative aspect on a higher level.

Example Script: *"Our technology is easy and gets leads for Agents, how do you feel about your Company's technology? Specifically how many leads you get? (If they say it's fine) Ok, let me ask you this, on a scale from 1 to 10, 10 being your database is running at the highest level (getting leads, everyone hears from you consistently), one being your database is on life support, how would you honestly rate it?*

Expert Tip: Goto Chapter on "Conviction/Building Bridges"

(If they say 7 or less *and they likely will*, how well can the tech be working for them ??)

"Oh wow, sorry to hear that but let me assure you it can be fixed. Let me ask you this, if I can show you an easy way to get your tech from a ___ to a ___ and it resulted in an extra 50k a year, would that be of value? **GET A FIRM YES** (conviction) and move on to next.

- *I want to make sure before we hang up that you are not just saying yes because it's easier in the moment but later you will cancel. Is this an appointment you can put in pen vs. pencil? In other words, if a buyer comes in from out of town at the last minute, can you work around it? Great! Because that would really blow up my schedule and I will make the same commitment to you, I will not cancel on you if something comes up, fair enough? Awesome, let me assure you then of a few things:*

1. *I won't pressure you to join my Company.*
2. *This will be strictly a coaching consult designed to help you net significantly more money.*
3. *All my consultations are an hour or less depending on your questions.*

Close: *"Fair enough? Great, see you ______________(confirm time/location)."*

Cold Call

- **Know their numbers script:** *"Hi_______________________, it's _______________________from _______________________, I just wanted to call you to congratulate you for a great year in _______(year), I see your business is up _____%! That's awesome! We had a great year too, my ___________office was up ______% (should be at least 15% higher)! Listen, we are both doing great so let's get together, I would love to hear about how you increased your business ______% and I will share how we went up ______% so that we can both keep the progress in______(year)!"*

- **Referred/co-op agent:** *"Hi________________, it's ________________from ___________, I saw you recently completed a transaction with (or went into contract with) my agent ______________ and I wanted to thank you for doing business with us, we really value working with professionals like yourself! Let me ask you a quick question, what's the biggest challenge in your business right now? Wow, we just did a training on (their issue)! Who is helping you with that (issue)? Well look, I don't mind, since you did such a great job with (agent), I coach with one Agent a week from outside my Company just to add value, let's get together!"*

- **Need to know you script:** *"Hi________________, it's ________________from ___________, I see you are local to me, and we never met although I have met many Agents in your sphere. Hey, listen, since we both play in the same sandbox, I would love to have a quick meeting with you to pick your brain about the market and share with you some of our best strategies our Agents are doing to get business as sort of a friendly "trade", fair enough?"*

Cold Call

On any cold call, start with announcing your title with something significant such as "Growth Director for 2nd Largest Real Estate Company in your region."

"I appreciate your time; do you have a minute for a BUSINESS call? Thank you, I will be brief."

"I am calling to congratulate you on your success with __________, I see you are up _____________. We are also up in that area (state a higher %). The business coach in me would love to pick your brain on what you are doing to get those results and I would be happy to share what we are doing here that should help you make even more money. I meet with two-three outside agents a week, I have some time this week on _____________, what does your schedule look like?"

(they say they can't)

"I understand, my time is valuable too and I don't want to waste your time as well as mine, but I certainly believe since we both play in the same sandbox that meeting would be beneficial, especially since I promise to keep recruiting you off the table and provide you with an idea or two that could make you an extra 20k a year. Assuming that was true, and I could give you a couple ideas to grow your business and make that kind of extra money, wouldn't that be a worthwhile 45 minutes?"

(they say yeah but I just can't do it this week)

"I understand, what does your schedule look like for next week? Consider this a million-dollar listing appointment where you have an opportunity to make a huge sum of money! I am sure that is an appointment you wouldn't cancel no matter what came up, right?"
(smile, laugh)

(if they still won't agree to meet)

"I appreciate that, well, let me ask can you this, would you share with me your biggest challenge right now in RE? (they state their challenge) *Yes! That is a challenge for many people! How about this, can I have permission to check in with you down the road and see how you are doing with* (restate challenge)*?"* (follow up in 30 days to check-in on their progress)

(they say "yes")

"Awesome, thank you for taking my call, I will email you a quick note, so you remember who I am and as always, don't hesitate to reach out if you need help with (restate challenge)."

Appendix C: Objection Handlers

Too busy: *"That's awesome, I love busy people! Let me ask you this, if you had an opportunity to attend a great listing appointment not knowing whether you would get it, would you attend? I figured you would say that! I get it, it's an opportunity to gain something…….. look, if I could put an extra $50k in your pocket year after year, would you consider that an opportunity to gain as well?"*

Happy where I am at: *"I am happy that you are happy, I love happy people! Listen, I don't know at this juncture if meeting with me involves leaving, I am just proposing that we get together, and I share some ideas to help your business. What's your biggest challenge? Great, if I can show you some strategies to help you with __________, wouldn't that be a good reason to meet?"*

Never Leaving: *"Fair enough. I am not sure that asking you to leave is something I would even feel comfortable with, I don't know you and you don't need me. Let me ask you this, do you work with a specific mortgage lender? Was there ever a time that you worked with another lender even though you thought you were set with your current lender? Sure, something changed, right? All I am proposing is we meet, and I share with you some things that are working for my Agents that could perhaps be something you can act on, asking you to leave your Company is off the table at this juncture, fair enough? Think of it this way, the worst case scenario is that you have another friend and a resource in the business! That way if something changes, just like it did with your lender, you have pre-screened another relationship!*

Non-Appointment Close out (can't get an appointment): *"So you aren't ready to meet, fair enough. Let me ask you this, if I follow up with you in a month, what is the one thing that you want to see progress on in your business that if you weren't making progress, it would not be ok with you?"*

Appendix D: Retention

*Using the Retention Ratio: Scenario (Agent wants to leave)

Step 1: Start with *"I understand you feel that <u>our</u> Company is holding you back and I understand what that must feel like. Can I ask you something directly? Would you agree that the Company is responsible for providing tools and support and the Agent is responsible for what they do with the tools? I am curious about something; do you mind if I ask you something? What % would you assign your success in this business based on your effort and what % would you place on tools and support?"*

(If they say Agent portion is 70% or less) *"I see, can I ask you some questions to understand why you feel that way? Thank you!"*

Step 2: Break out your questions and start to find the problem in their business like you do with a recruit, start fishing!

Example: *Who does the stuff in your business (leverage issue)? How would you rate your database from a scale from 1 to 10? Etc.*

Step 3: Get them to admit to a re-calibrate. *"Can I ask you the same question I asked you earlier……..?"*

Step 4: Close it out. *"Thank you for your vulnerability, I think we identified what we need to work on for you to hit your goals. The good news is that we have the solutions to (stated problem), let's see what that looks like, fair enough?"*

Appendix E:
Pre-Prospecting Best Practices

- **Prepare your listing prior to your session.**
- **Put a note on your door letting visitors know you are prospecting.**
- **Read your vision/mission statement.**
- **Smile and have gratitude in your heart.**

Appendix F:
"Onboarding Best Practices"

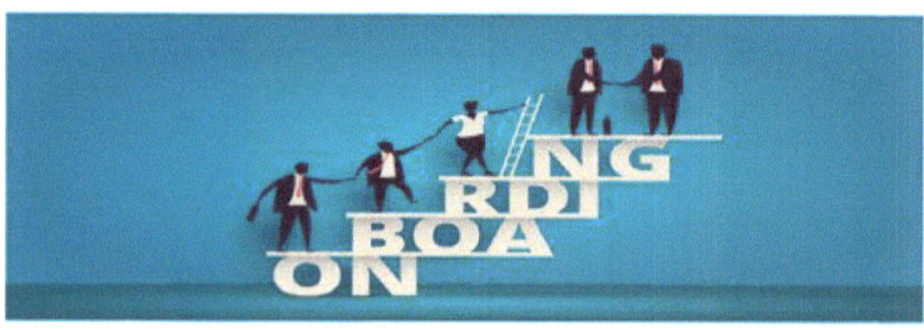

It is critical to "show" a step-by-step plan to assure Agents coming to your company that you have a well-thought-out plan. A defined plan not only speaks to the analytic nature of people, but it also reduces the perceived "disruption" an Agent feels.

"Set-up:" Introduce your "Soft-Landing" Program (transition plan) after the <u>conviction.</u>

"I am truly excited for your future with our Company and to minimize any of the normal disruptions in the move in progress, we have a program we call "The Soft Landing" that all our top Agents follow in order to expedite your success plan with our Company."

Highlights of "The Soft Landing" Transition Plan

Activity Notes:

- Database transfer assistance _____________________
- Business cards ordered__________________________
- New "headshot" provided_______________________
- CRM set-up assistance_________________________
- Website established____________________________
- Office orientation_____________________________
- Client Announcement campaign________________
- Office Welcome Announcement_________________
- Social Media Announcement____________________
- 30 Day Coaching Appointment_________________

Appendix G:
Handling Adversity: New Constitution

- Attitude is a choice, things that are out of your control will happen anyway.
- Every setback presents an opportunity to get further in your career/development.
- Your lack of ability to thrive during a setback shines a light on your current skill level.
- We don't know what others are thinking, assigning meaning to other people's thoughts takes away from positive feelings.
- Feeling anger over what you think others are saying gives credit to their limitations.

- Most people only have fleeting thoughts about you, having pro-longed dialogue in your head about what you think they are saying makes you weaker.
- Having grace in moments of failure project attractiveness and respect.
- Never lash out, it only serves to weaken your perceived position. Always take time to respond to conflict.
- Replace thoughts of resentment with thoughts of gratitude.
- Thank often, lead with love.